Confusion

Charleston, SC
www.PalmettoPublishing.com

Confusion
Copyright © 2023 by Marvin R. Lowery

All rights reserved

No portion of this book may be reproduced, stored in a retrieval system, or transmitted in any form by any means–electronic, mechanical, photocopy, recording, or other–except for brief quotations in printed reviews, without prior permission of the author.

First Edition

Paperback ISBN: 979-8-8229-1045-4

Confusion

Marvin R. Lowery

Table of Contents

Beginning 2

Healing 3

Growing 4

Learning 5

Learning 2 7

Champion 8

Dimension 9

The Digest 10

Uncanny 12

Uncertainty 13

Discomposure 14

Puzzlement 15

IGNORANCE 17

Shock 18

Upheaval 19

Show out 20

Exercise 22

Strength 23

Boulder 24

Gain 25

Scream 27

Listen 28

Actor 29

Do Re Mi False 30

Disillusion 32

Virus 33

Pictures 34

Phrase 35

Traveling Voice 37

Radio 38

Sing Until You Can't Breathe . . . 39

Disparity 40

Flows 42

Walled off 43

Peroration 44

Beginning

Once a being is born it develops a conscience

Absorbing knowledge from its domain

Using all five senses, gets rid of the nonsense

With all of the information it has attained

Any more excessive use could cause a strain

Making that being tired and fatigued

Producing what is called a scatterbrain

For once a being has become intrigued

It will seek to learn moro and more

Trying to make sense of its world

So that it will never become bored

The being will no longer stay furled

As its mind rotates, becoming whirled

While the being lives and grows

Its perception will become birled

Just like oceans individual beliefs will ebb and flow

Until the being is secure in itself

And knows what it truly is

The apprehension gained will be put on a shelf

Till the time of the ultimate quiz

The being must be quiet until it's time to share its biz

Becoming aware of its nature

Thoroughly constructing an in-depth analysis

The being's life will never waver

As long as it follows its heart

Being true with all of its morals

The goal will always be to reach its mark

And the being can rest on its laurels

Healing

There once was a wise man who said that anything broken can always be fixed;
given enough time, healing, and patience.
There once was a student who was ambitious
and never wanted to wait to heal;
So, he used herbs and medicine to heal faster.

A person's choice is his or hers alone.

The wise man took it slow and waited to heal,
always finding joy in the small things.
He learned new skills to pass the time,
while also watching the birds fly by.
The student decided he didn't want to wait;
he tried to find a way to heal faster.
He lost a better opportunity for personal growth,
since he didn't like for time to impose.

A person's choice is his or hers alone.

The wise man learned more and more,
gaining more knowledge and skills.
The student wasted time rushing to heal,
never understanding that healing takes time.
As one lets go of pain, new fortunes arise.
Holding on to an old pain causes only stress and sorrow.

A persons choice is his or hers alone.

Growing

When people want to master a skill bad enough,
they will set a schedule to wake in the morning dew.
Conforming to that schedule can be tough;
but being consistent can make dreams come true.

So, why is it hard to conform to a schedule?
Why is it hard for an entrepreneur to start a business?
Maybe, some never seek to be successful.
Maybe, some people suffer from an illness.

An illness of the mind that seeks to stop
an ongoing narrative in a person's head that says you won't succeed.
When seeking success to reach the top,
It may be best to start by taking the lead.

Learn from life and be happy with who you are;
believing that something important awaits.
People will see they can go far;
this is how to become one of the greats.

So, even though one might struggle and be confused,
they can always go far when waking in the morning dew.

Learning

Acquiring an ability

always takes time,

requiring some patience.

Is resting always

the best option?

Learning 2

Gaining proficiency at a task will always take time.
An individual will want to even give up sometimes.
In the darkest of nights there will always be a sun.
A sun that shines so bright it makes a person get up and run.
For if one never runs, he or she will never get to climb.

At the top of a mountain is where dreams unfold;
where a warrior can gain the upper hand and take control.
Leaving unhealthy thoughts and negatives behind;
Standing at the top shows how limits are defined.
Shouting out at the world the warrior's message is told.

Champion

When a bee flies off in the sky
It never loses sight of its goal
Its life's path to never deny
For the path is what makes it whole

What goals can humans achieve;
 being able to create or write?
A goal as one's resolution,
once executed creates joy and excites.

Champions need to let go of haters
and develop and grow his or her own path.
Ultimately, becoming their own exceptional creators.

Dimension

A path is created, but only one person goes through.

He takes off going leftfootrightintothelane.

Ta ki

Ng ev

Er yt

Hi ng

In st

Ri de

Th ee

nd is

ne ar

The journey is never complete.

The Digest

For all we know paper comes from tree leaves,

but paper can also be made from grass.

This makes the statement, "Money doesn't grow on trees", ambivalent.

See, money forms at the cost of plant fibers being interwoven,

 making a single bill that can support the masses.

Since each dollar bill is made from the same material;

is a dollar simply a way for others to have control?

If people don't have money, they can't pay for many things.

The issue of money problems seems to be hysterical.

It seems that now making money is a person's end goal.

However, if money is created without government compliance; then it's not legal.

Uncanny

When a baby bird learns how to fly

When a toddler takes his first steps

The triumph was from how the mind started to prep.

There was no hesitation, nor a wondering of why.

It had to be learned, it had to be done.

For if a living thing cannot move its life could be done

Once a person grows older, indecision creeps in

Always wondering why it should do this.... where, what, and when?

Once a skill is learned; for questions, there will be none.

Uncertainty

There is uncertainty in everything,

from how one wakes up in the morning

and how one goes to sleep for the night.

No one knows everything or anything.

There is no sound, no alert, no warning.

People just have to believe in themselves; take flight.

If people didn't believe in themselves; we would have no sports.

No trophies, no honorable mentions, no education.

No one would ever want to kick the field goal.

For better or for worse, the world needs disarray in order to not fall short.

The disarray and the doubt that comes with it all encompasses uncertainty.

Discomposure

Some circumstances seem to cause a commotion,

such as how a dog barks at a stranger's introduction.

When people hold all their anger in, it turns into a rage—explosion,

losing sight of what's going on in the world and how things are interwoven.

If people just chose to let go and deal with all their emotions,

maybe it wouldn't feel like their world was experiencing an implosion.

In order to appear very well composed,

a long hard look in the mirror could change the negative notions.

Puzzlement

Ponder for a moment a flower in a field,

 it does more than just stay in place.

Flowers bring us oxygen to help us breathe and heal.

Some people tend to stay in one place.

Some, however, decide to do more and live life like it's a race.

Is it possible to do both instead of one versus the other?

For if one can learn to do both, then a wonderful world is discovered.

It can make a person bewildered by how fast life goes.

If people take the time to relax, more wonders will be uncovered.

SO, take some time to be yourself and grow up looking like a rose.

IGNORANCE

Knowledge is power; so libraries were built.

However; many people don't use libraries as much these days.

Information can be found on a phone or computer easily.

Yet, ignorance is still very profound in society today.

There are many different articles and publications: however; knowledge has been refused.

Knowledge isn't real unless people learn things for themselves.

Even though other forms of mass media exist; no one believes anything

unless it coincides with their beliefs and is on their phone or computer.

Ignorance will prevail unless people start researching, reading, and learning from every source possible.

Shock

Picture a runner at the start of race,
no time for thinking, just keeping his head in the game;
always focused on coming in first, hearing people scream his name.
What if winning or being successful wasn't something to be chased?

In elementary school, it was said that a turtle can survive by staying focused on one goal.
The rabbit doesn't survive because of ego, showboating, or distraction.
Looking back now, that story seems to have some pot holes.
Today, people focus on more than one job just to stay in action.

Why is it we are taught to focus on one thing instead of multiple passions?
Would doing so many different things end up causing a bad reaction?
When pursuing your own dream, the race is never lost.

Upheaval

Jumping, jumping from one thing to the next.

They say you can do what you want when you're older.

However; first you need to pass a bunch of tests.

Tests seem to show how good a person is at following someone else's rules.

Tests will never explain how to be your own boss; using your own tools.

It's an uphill battle to get ones dreams to come to fruition.

The way we are taught is all about following the system.

Why is it that students aren't taught about taxes, stocks, or retirement plans early?

If everyone learned more than just the basic one, twos and threes;

imagine for a second how much better the world could be.

Show out

A creative and an entrepreneur goes to far in life and moves way too fast.

Moving too fast for whom exactly? Each life is different from the other.

So why is one person annoyed by another's progress?

Is it because the courageous person's life doesn't fit in with another person's goals?

This is never the way life works; that's not how life unfolds.

So to those who are always doing their very best– live the life of your dreams.

and keep showing out!!!

Exercise

Most people exercise to get fit and healthy

Some, however, say they don't have the time.

Others say working out is past their prime.

Some people say it's only for the wealthy

Bosses usually say spend your time wisely

ALWAYS OVERWORKED MAKING EXERCISE HIGHLY UNLIKELY!!

Strength

Going to the gym may sometimes seem perplexed

by the different exercise equipment and ways to use them.

This goes for everyday life when thinking about what's next;

such as getting on a bus not knowing where to sit.

 Life is not as confusing as it seems.

Simply look under the veil; it's all natural.

Elder generations and those who don't explore think life moves off of one theme.

 Life has many plays, many struggles.

Each person carries a different weight; some are unfathomable.

 If each person learned to let go of that theme, that struggle;

the world might eventually become a better place for all.

Don't hide behind a mask and look for trouble.

Find the inner strength to accept each other.

 There won't be a need for a wall.

Boulder

How heavy is a weight in one's life?
Does it way them down, cause strife?
Why do people carry so much weight?
Why not let go before it's too late?

A weight is something that's meant to be moved;
through pain and perseverance strength is improved.
A weight on the mind is usually cruel.
Until the weight is dropped, the mind is a useless tool.

Break barriers at work, break barriers at the gym;
once home and alone, a person's mind becomes a hindrance.
The agony of the brain is actually worse than a broken limb.
Learn to drop that weight and gain independence.

Gain

Aspiring to be strong is a natural thing,
staying in shape until one becomes a king.

What happens if a person is too strong?
Does it make it harder for a person to get along?

Sometimes life makes it harder to let your guard down.
By letting your guard down, you just might drown.

Life can have its complications.
People go to school to learn communications;
to be the only species that can communicate with words.
Sometimes those words go unheard.

If people actually tried to understand one another;
maybe THERE wouldn't be people stealing from each other.

Some people don't care at all and life just goes on,
maybe this why they just feel a need to be strong.

Scream

Stand on top of a hill and what do you hear?

The sound of the world travels in the air.

The sound is so magnificent, it makes one aware;

aware of glorious nature, nothing to fear.

Is nature the only sound that can bring about peace?

If a person turns his head, he can hear a lot.

The sound of a fan brings coolness for the day.

The sounds of food slow cooking in a big pot;

causes people to relax, knowing they are not going to starve.

If someone isn't hungry, a work of art can be carved.

Sometimes an artist may go hungry,

making him want to scream to the top of his lungs.

The artist is creating new works for those to see.

Artists want to create until their final bell is rung.

Listen

A sense that most people have is the ability to hear.

Hearing someone isn't the same as understanding.

In order to understand each other, one must be sincere.

However, there are those who can't get over their own traumas; causing misunderstandings.

An incident in one person's life may be different than another's life.

If a person has basic empathy and sympathy for his own mother and brother;

why is there often no sympathy and compassion for a person of a different color?

Learning about someone else's life could get rid of all stressors.

No one is ever born not liking someone else; it's taught and this is what creates chaos.

Have sympathy and compassion, one in the same; learn about your neighbor.

Learning about differences can make life much greater.

There doesn't need to be confusion about other people and how they live.

Just listening can make the world better.

Actor

What's the purpose of an actor's job?...... speak truth, fiction, or bring fantasies to life?
People see plays, watch tv, and movies; but when fiction is reality, people are filled with strife.

IS life not fantasy in and of itself? ...just being alive and awestruck by nature.
When fiction becomes a reality, some people will begin to question... is it real or fiction?
Aren't we all actors?
We perform differently in our jobs.
Is that who we really are?
Are we just performing...actors?

Do Re Mi False

Everything in life begins with a start.

People wonder how their story ends.

However; life wasn't meant to be studied like a math chart.

Living life in the present is how one can be content.

Charging at life head on is what some people recommend.

If a thought tends to linger way too long;

The inner voice in the head starts to condescend.

This type of negative thinking shouldn't be prolonged;

because a lot of bad thoughts can lead to false hope.

This leaves a person singing do re mi say it isn't so.

So, how does one get rid of their negative thoughts and vibes?

THE only thing that works is to be positive,

Start telling yourself better things;

and see how much you'll gain.

Disillusion

The world is constantly spinning around and around.

Life on earth often turns to forms of disarray.

The world seems so different. Are people standing on solid ground?

Some people don't believe the truth even when heavily displayed.

This is evident in news shows that discuss topics of the day.

Why is one disillusioned from how he was raised?

He may be distant from the world because his thoughts are closed.

Is there a way for one to get over his past and learn to simply relax?

If suggesting to another he should go on vacation, would it be opposed?

Many people don't like the opinions of others, even when it's known to be a suggestion.

It's difficult to talk about an idea without another thinking this is an order being told.

How will the world continue if people can't learn to effectively communicate?

It seems the only thing that one can do is patiently sit down and wait.

Virus

PEOPLE GET SICK AND BECOME HURT DAY IN AND DAY OUT
Sometimes the pain of sickness makes one start to shout!

Even though there is pain; there is also beauty.
Love is shown by those who know you.

Even though a virus may take a life;
keep your head held high and live life without strife.

There are ways to make the most of a moment.
Take the time to find enjoyment.

It's hard to lose a loved one, everyone has been there.
What's more important is how that time was shared.

If life is never cherished, a heart may perish.
Through every struggle; it's always important to show love and spread it.

Pictures

Pictures speak a thousand words that's often said;

take a look at a picture and a hidden message is never read.

Someone may look at a picture and see a person smiling.

What is going on behind the picture, what's hiding?

Emotion is shown in every picture a person takes.

This creates a story that another wants to partake.

As people, we often create unusual storylines;

like a bird in the sky showing freedom, never confined.

After a picture is taken the story stops moving;

there is no more challenge to convey a story that's pursuing.

Why does there always have to be a story within everything done?

A story tells a lot about a person, such as who and what they love.

Take a picture every now and then.

In the future you'll want to look back at where you've been.

Phrase

A poet is able to constantly turn everyday things

into the most simplest of phrases with few syllables.

The world may look at a poem and think;

but a phrase is interpreted differently by individuals.

Poems are never meant to be taken too literal.

Poems are just meant to be a helping guide;

filled with thoughts and emotions to open one's eyes.

Poems bring meanings out of simple things; nowhere to hide.

Traveling Voice

A voice can travel 180 meters in still air.
A person only speaks when someone else is there.
The pain of speaking when no one is listening brings despair.
Often times a person may speak because he is unaware.

A deaf man can't hear anyone; but still seeks to communicate.
Standing by and having patience for someone else is a long wait.
A blind man can't see, so he will slowly listen to sounds to help locate.
Locate his surroundings to find friends who know his condition and can relate.

 Why is it that people who can see and speak,
refuse to see and hear the beauty in life?
With no illness or disability, some people let life pass by;
until they get sick themselves and start to cry.
This has never happened to them before; they don't take life by the wings
......AND FLY

Radio

Voices and songs on the radio come and go

as they continuously move forward into one path.

The radio helps people to stay awake, not wreck on the metro.

If songs were never played, a person might flip their cargo.

If one isn't focused, there may be bad aftermath.

Radio is played in stores to calm a customer's mood in line.

If the customer gets to upset, he might commit a crime.

Why is it that sound is so crucial to every living being?

Does sound somehow relax the mind; make one feel freeing?

As soon as the world stops, sound is gone.

People turn to darkness; nothing else for their emotions to act upon.

If a person can master being alone in silence;

that person might not commit acts of violence.

RELAX

Sing Until You Can't Breathe

Sing until you can't breathe, let the music move you.

Let the sounds seep into your skin; be the drug in your system.

It's okay to take time for yourself; let the coffee brew.

Feeling good about yourself can relax the nervous system.

If you're down and out and music isn't for you,

go and listen to the sounds of nature.

No need to hold on to stress and anger,

relaxing to the sound of the world can make your soul anew.

So Sing Until you can't breathe, let the music move you.

Let the sounds seep into your skin; be the drug in your system.

Whatever it is that relaxes you, is good for you.

Take some time for yourself; let the coffee brew.

Disparity

The world is constantly in a state of disparity
with talks about equality and equity.
If people looked from the outside in,
would they see where disparity begins?

Equality and equity are largely two different things.
One seeks to have everyone have the same opportunities;
the other seeks to bring about lasting change.
Equality doesn't take account for ambiguities.

One person may have no legs, another no eyes.
Is equal opportunity given for those whose condition
makes a job opportunity constantly denied?
In order to have the same opportunities,
people must first change their position and think about another's condition.

Flows

Water Flows, water falls
Water flows down a river
Giving life to everything
Water is considered a life giver
For no plant or being can survive
Without water constantly consumed
Without water, is one even alive?

What makes a person live without water
A purpose that's bigger than what they imagine
Maybe the purpose is being a writer or author
Living for a reason is what fuels a passion
If people don't know their purpose; they may become agitated
Lash out at others who are living their dreams
Because they become so angry and feel that their life is unvalidated
They never take into account that maybe their dreams have different streams
Because to know ones passion isn't a race to find
The biggest and most rewarding dreams take their time
To come to fruition so one must relax
Until they get their premonition.

Walled off

There are often many barriers that keep people from enjoying life

A person may be in the best mood ever, but get pulled to the side like a lever

These things that try to trap someone's life becomes annoying

However, if people never experienced some annoyance, they wouldn't know enjoyment

Everyone goes through pain and agony, so most can relate

It's just how life works; there's no need to get mad and be full of hate

If people take the time to realize things happen to everyone

They wouldn't take their frustrations out on others

Life often works in mysterious ways and no one knows why

not knowing one's purpose or reason for hurting

 one should still cheer, so don't constantly stay upset

 because part of your life got walled down

There are other paths still; like kicking that wall down, looking beyond the pain, and reversing that frown.

Peroration

Throughout the world there is always a form of confusion;
something to make people sit down and think.
Whether it be mirror or warped refraction of water causing an illusion,
while being skeptical and bewildered could be a waste of time, it's best to have a drink.
Trying to understand the happenings of the world causes one's mind to grow, not shrink.
If one simply sits there and doesn't contemplate anything, there is no personal growth.
Trying to not make sense of certain things goes against human instinct.

Even though it's hard to admit, no one can really fly like a bird.
Flying isn't the only path to actually having true freedom.
Having a clear and open mind lets thoughts be heard.
Freedom has many forms that lets one create his own kingdom;
but he must let go of unduly thoughts, enjoy the seasons like spring.
Life is something people only have one chance at having.
Let go of irritations and enjoy the bewilderment of life some.
Time is fleeting and moving so fast; it even starts to move by people passing.

With every disparity that one goes through there's always beauty at the end,
to achieve the ending of one's own unique journey; it has to begin.

www.ingramcontent.com/pod-product-compliance
Lightning Source LLC
LaVergne TN
LVHW081458060526
838201LV00057BA/3071